9. 50

THE FORESTS

THIS EARTH OF OURS

Mel Higginson

The Rourke Corporation, Inc.
Vero Beach, Florida 32964

Edited by Sandra A. Robinson

PHOTO CREDITS
© Mel Higginson: cover, title page, pages 4, 7, 12, 15, 17;
© James P. Rowan: pages 8, 13, 18, 21; © Frank Balthis: page 10

Library of Congress Cataloging-in-Publication Data

Higginson, Mel, 1942-
    The forests / by Mel Higginson.
    p. cm. — (This earth of ours)
    Includes index.
    ISBN 0-86593-382-0
    1. Forest ecology—Juvenile literature. 2. Forests and forestry—
Juvenile literature. [1. Forest ecology. 2. Ecology.] I. Title.
II. Series: Higginson, Mel, 1942-   This earth of ours.
QH541.5F6H54   1994
574.5'2642—dc20   94-9405
                                                        CIP
                                                        AC
Printed in the USA

TABLE OF CONTENTS

FORESTS

Forests are heavily wooded areas that cover much of the world's land.

Forests are **habitats,** or homes, for many plants and animals. Small groups of people still live in some of the world's most **remote** forests.

Forests provide people with valuable wood products. Forest plants also help keep soil in place, clean the air and control air temperatures.

Early morning sunlight pours through the branches of hemlock trees in a Vermont forest

WHERE FORESTS ARE

Forests are on every continent except Antarctica. Forests develop wherever trees can grow. Trees need firm, fertile soil and several inches of rainfall each year.

In North America, much of eastern Canada and the eastern United States are covered by forest. Many of the mountain slopes in the West are forested, too.

The world's tallest and mightiest trees are the redwoods and sequoias of northern California.

One of the world's greatest forests is the tropical rain forest along the Amazon River in South America.

The world's tallest trees — mighty redwoods — stand tall in northern California's Redwood National Park

KINDS OF FORESTS

Forests are not all alike. Scientists separate forests by the kinds of trees that grow in them.

North America alone has several different kinds of forests. Part of Mexico is covered by tropical rain forest.

In other parts of North America, forests are mostly needle-leaved trees or broad-leaved trees. Pines and spruces are needle-leaved trees. Maples, beech and oak are common broad-leaved trees. Some of their leaves change to bright colors before dropping in the fall.

The tropical rain forest — like this one in Borneo — is a rich habitat for plants and animals

LIFE IN THE FORESTS

Forests are habitats for more than trees. Vines, shrubs, flowers, mosses, ferns and other plants grow below and sometimes among the trees.

Birds live among the shrubs and branches of the forest. Many mammals live in the forest. Some live in the trees. Others live on the forest floor.

Some of the animals of the world's forests are chimpanzees, gorillas, black bears, jaguars and squirrels. Snakes, toads, tree frogs and many kinds of smaller animals live in forests, too.

A gorilla peers through the leaves of a mountain forest in Rwanda, Africa

The lynx prowls the northern forests of Europe, Asia and North America

*Huron Indians used to live in "longhouses"
built of wood and bark in eastern Canada*

HOW ANIMALS LIVE IN THE FOREST

Many forest animals are skilled climbers. Tree squirrels are not fast runners, and they can't dig holes for hiding. However, they are good climbers, just like pine **martens,** monkeys and certain forest snakes.

Birds that live in the forest can perch easily on branches. Most forest birds build their nests in shrubs or trees.

14

The weasel of the treetops, this speedy pine marten chases — and catches — pine squirrels in northern forests

A FOREST ANIMAL: THE WOODPECKER

Each animal of the forest has special tools to use in the forest. Woodpeckers, for example, have special bills to chip wood and drill holes in trees. Woodpecker feet are specially shaped for clinging on bark while the bird hammers the tree.

Most of a woodpecker's food is the insects it finds by drilling in trees. The woodpecker nests in holes it makes. The holes are also used by other forest creatures.

The red-headed woodpecker is perfectly suited to life in a forest habitat

PEOPLE WHO LIVE IN THE FORESTS

A few groups of **tribal** people still live in forests far away from cities. A group of **pygmies** in Africa calls itself "children of the forest." Other tribes live in the warm forests of Asia and South America. Many years ago, several tribes of Native Americans lived in the forests of North America.

True forest tribes are becoming rare. Many of the last, large tropical rain forests where they live are being cut down.

The cutting and burning of rain forests for farmland has made true forest tribes scarce

HOW PEOPLE LIVE IN FORESTS

The **culture,** or way of life, of forest tribes depends upon the health of the forest. The forest provides the things they need to live. Forest people make homes of logs and leaves. They use forest plants to make medicines, too.

Forest people have learned to move quietly through forests. They use bows and arrows, darts and snares to hunt forest animals. In South America, certain tribes dip their hunting arrows in poisons taken from the bodies of forest frogs. The frogs are called poison-arrow frogs.

Some South American forest tribes dip their hunting arrows in the poison of colorful poison-arrow frogs

THE FOREST COMMUNITY

The plants and animals of a forest live together in a natural community. Each member of the community depends upon the others in some way.

Forest plants make homes and hiding places for animals. They also provide food for many animals. Oak trees, for example, drop the acorns that wild turkeys, deer and squirrels love.

Plant-eating animals become the **prey,** or food, of **predators** like lynxes, martens and fox snakes.

Glossary

culture (KULT cher) — a group of people's way of life

habitat (HAB uh tat) — the special kind of area where an animal lives, such as *forest*

marten (MART in) — a tree-climbing member of the weasel and otter family

predator (PRED uh tor) — an animal that kills other animals for food

prey (PRAY) — an animal killed by another animal for food

pygmy (PIG me) — a group of small, forest-dwelling people in Africa

remote (re MOTE) — somewhere far away or out-of-the-way

tribal (TRI bull) — relating to a tribe of people

INDEX